W9-AMY-798

Big Horses, Little Horses

A Visual Guide to the World's Horses and Ponies

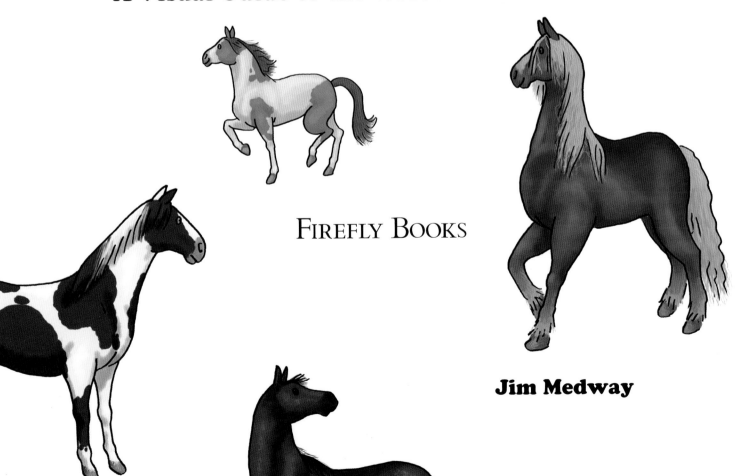

FIREFLY BOOKS

Jim Medway

Contents

North American Horses

Many of the world's greatest horse breeds from the United States and Canada, including the Tennessee Walker, the Mustang, and the American Quarter Horse. 4

British and Irish Horses

A variety of celebrated breeds, from the tiny Shetland Pony to the massive Shire. 9

European Horses

Famous breeds from the Scandinavian north to the Mediterranean south, such as the Lipizzaner, Friesian, and Andalusian. 12

Asian Horses

World Horses

Foals

Horse Breed Index

North American Horses

Mustang

Morab

Paso Fino

Chincoteague

Marsh Tacky

Florida Cracker

National Show
Horse

American Curly

American
Quarter Horse

American
Saddlebred

Lippitt Morgan

Canadian
Sport

Standardbred

North American Horses (continued)

Racking Horse

Kentucky Mountain

Spotted Saddle

Nokota

North American Single-Footing

Moyle

Morgan

Rocky
Mountain

Mountain
Pleasure

Tennessee
Walker

Missouri
Fox Trotter

Canadian Horse

American
Paint

North American Horses (continued)

McCurdy Plantation

Colorado Ranger

American Cream Draft

Appaloosa

Palomino

Newfoundland Pony

British and Irish Horses

Cleveland Bay

Clydesdale

Fell Pony

Eriskay Pony

Welsh Mountain Pony

Hackney

Welsh Cob Pony

British and Irish Horses (continued)

Kerry Bog Pony

Exmoor Pony

Connemara

Shire

Dartmoor Pony

Suffolk Punch

Dales Pony

New Forest Pony

Irish Sport

English Thoroughbred

Shetland Pony

Irish Draft

Highland Pony

European Horses

Heck

Camargue

Aegidienberger

Finnhorse

Noriker

Dutch Harness

Lusitano

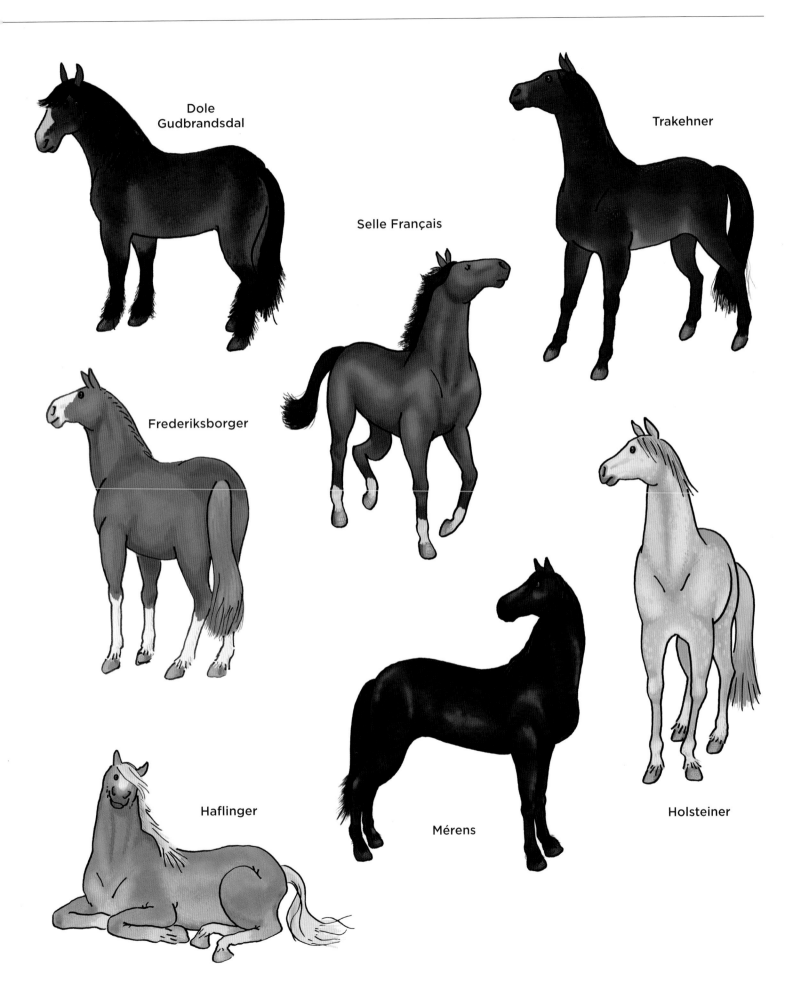

Dole
Gudbrandsdal

Trakehner

Selle Français

Frederiksborger

Holsteiner

Haflinger

Mérens

European Horses (continued)

Spanish Jennet

North Swedish

Friesian

Miniature

Icelandic

Ardennes

Black Forest

Bardigiano

Andalusian

Dülmen Pony

Kladruber

Percheron

Spanish
Mustang

Murgese

European Horses (continued)

Belgian Warmblood

Estonian

Breton

Fjord

Gotland Pony

Jutland

Danish Warmblood

Württemberger

Swedish Warmblood

Comtois

Boulonnais

Italian Heavy Draft

Dutch Warmblood

Bavarian

European Horses (continued)

Oldenburg

Belgian Draft

Freiberger

Lipizzaner

Sorraia

Faroe Pony

Westphalian

Norman Cob

Menorquín

Shagya Arabian

Knabstrupper

Nordlandshest

Pottok

Maremmano

Hanoverian

Asian Horses

Miyako

Karabakh

Przewalski's
Horse

Altai

Lokai

Hequ

Jeju

Orlov Trotter

Kiso

Russian Trotter

Yonaguni

Mongolian

Misaki

Asian Horses (continued)

Caspian

Kabardin

Vyatka

Akhal-Teke

Marwari

Novokirghiz

Russian Don

Arabian

Java Pony

Karabair

Kathiawari

Tersk

Budenny

World Horses

Criollo

Mangalarga
Marchador

Azteca

Australian
Draft

Brumby

Chilean
Corralero

Boerperd

Falabella

Galiceno

Peruvian Paso

Barb

Kaimanawa

Australian
Stock

Dongola

Campolina

Foals

English
Thoroughbred

Andalusian

American
Paint

Arabian

Irish Draft

Friesian

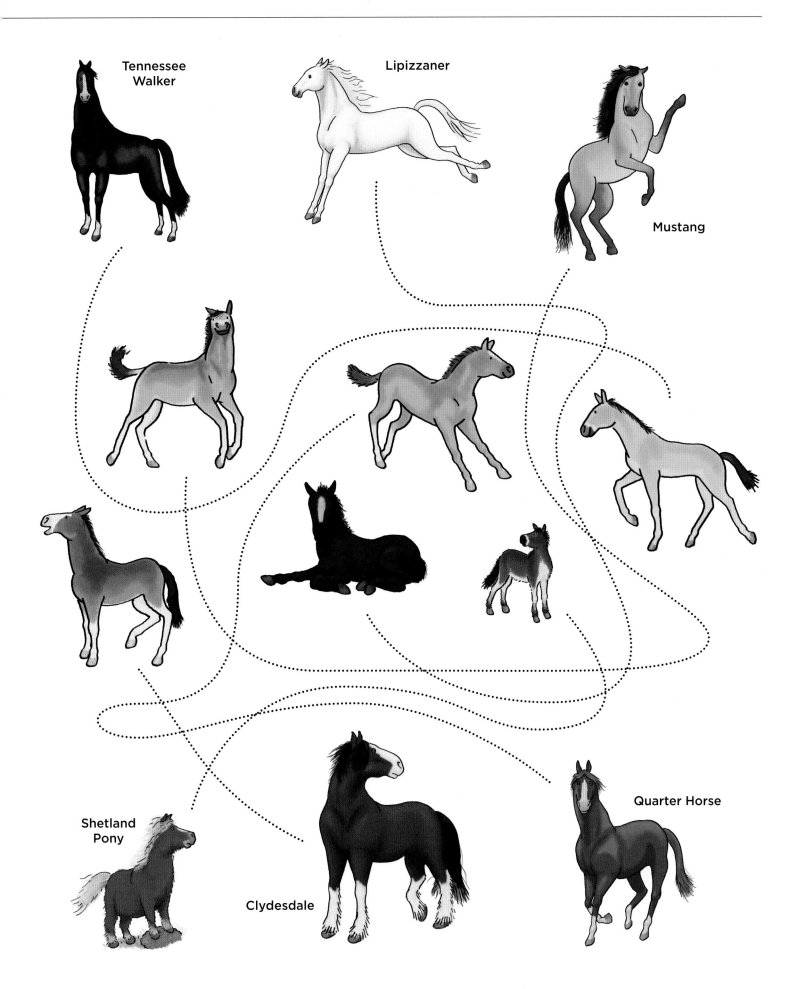

Tennessee Walker

Lipizzaner

Mustang

Shetland Pony

Clydesdale

Quarter Horse

Horse Breeds

Aegidienberger
This little horse is a cross between an Icelandic Horse and a Peruvian Paso. 12

Akhal-Teke
From Turkmenistan in Asia, this sleek breed is famous for its ultra-glossy coat, which has an almost metallic sheen. 22

Altai
Bred in the Altai Mountains of Central Asia, this horse used to be ridden by the area's nomads and tribesmen. 20

American Cream Draft
These cream-colored horses all have white manes and tails. When they are born they have white eyes, which change to amber as they age. 8

American Curly
Native American tribes, the Sioux and the Crow, are known to have ridden the American Curly breed. 5

American Paint
This American horse breed is recognized by its distinctive markings, which look like dark-colored paint spots or splashes. 7, 26

American Quarter Horse
Probably the most popular horse breed in the United States, the Quarter Horse is often used as a racehorse and for western pleasure rides — western-style competitions at horse shows. At short distances, it is the fastest horse in the world. 5, 27

American Saddlebred
The breed was once known as the Kentucky Saddler. Its smooth ride and strong stamina meant that farmers could ride from dawn till dusk in comfort. 5

Andalusian
Usually grey, the Andalusian is one of the oldest horse breeds. Originally used as a warhorse, it is noted for its thick mane and tail. It was prized by Spanish nobles. 15, 26

Andalusian

Appaloosa
Identified by its spotted coat pattern and sparse mane and tail, this American breed is tough and independent. It makes an excellent trail horse. 8

Arabian
From the deserts of the Arabian Peninsula, this breed is one of the oldest in the world. It is renowned for its strength, speed, and endurance. 23, 26

Ardennes
A very old breed, this draft horse from Belgium is believed to have existed in ancient Roman times. 14

Australian Draft
Bred from four other draft horses — Shire, Percheron, Clydesdale, and Suffolk Punch — this breed was developed by colonists in Australia. 24

Australian Stock
The Stock is a versatile breed that can be used for polo, showjumping, dressage, endurance, and eventing, as well as stock work (working with livestock, particularly cattle). 25

Azteca
This Mexican horse was first bred in the 1970s by mixing an American Quarter Horse with an Andalusian. 24

Barb
These horses from North Africa were once used for close-combat fighting. Barbs are agile and can stop and change direction quickly. 25

Bardigiano
From the mountains of Emilia Romagna in northern Italy, this small horse is adapted to work in steep and rough terrain. 15

Bavarian
Solid dark in color, this German horse is used for showjumping and dressage. 17

Belgian Draft
The huge, gentle-spirited Belgian Draft has a chestnut coat and white mane and tail. 18

Belgian Warmblood
"Big Ben", a Belgian Warmblood born in Belgium, became one of Canada's most famous showjumping horses in the 1980s. Warmbloods are a group of middleweight horses; heavy draft horses such as the Shire and Clydesdale are described as coldbloods. 16

Black Forest
From the Black Forest in Germany, this stocky horse has a thick mane and tail, both light flaxen in color. Its body is deep chestnut. 14

Boerperd
The Boerperd was recreated from the now extinct Cape Horse in South Africa. The Cape Horse used to be a favorite of Boer farmers. 24

Boulonnais
A draft horse from France, the breed is also known as the White Marble Horse because of its grey color. 17

Breton
A strong horse, the Breton has muscular legs and is good for endurance riding. It is normally chestnut. 16

Brumby
A free-roaming feral horse in Australia, the Brumby is descended from lost or escaped horses that European settlers brought with them in the 19th century. 24

Budenny
The Budenny or Budyonny was developed by the Russian cavalry after World War I by mixing Thoroughbreds with Russian Dons. 23

Camargue
These semi-wild horses come from the Camargue, a wetland area at the mouth of the river Rhône in France. At birth they are brown, but they turn white when they are about four years old. 12

Campolina
From Brazil, the Campolina is a gaited horse, meaning it can perform one of the smooth-to-ride, intermediate-speed, four-beat gaits called "ambling gaits". It has a distinct rounded head. 25

Canadian
This horse is believed to be descended from horses first brought to North American by the French King Louis XIV in the late 1600s. 7

Canadian Sport
The breed was created by mixing Canadian farm horses with English Thoroughbreds. 5

Caspian
This ancient breed from northern Iran is a horse, not a pony, despite its small size. It is believed to have been the forerunner of the Arabian Horse. 22

Chilean Corralero
The oldest horse breed in South America, the Corralero has a thick coat and strong hooves, and is suited to living in both hot and cold climates. 24

Chincoteague
These ponies live on the barrier island of Assateague in Maryland and Virginia, in the United States. They graze on beach and marsh grasses. 4

Cleveland Bay
This rare breed is the oldest in England. From Cleveland in Yorkshire, it is always bay (reddish-brown) in color with a black mane, tail, and lower legs. The British Royal Family still use Cleveland Bays to pull carriages in royal processions. 9

Clydesdale
The noble and brave Clydesdale is one of the most popular draft horses in the world. It has silky feathers (hair) behind its hooves and white marks on its nose and feet. 9, 27

Colorado Ranger
First bred on the open range in Colorado in the United States, this horse's origins can be traced to two horses, an Arabian called Leopold and a Barb called Linden Tree, that were given to General Ulysses S. Grant by the Sultan of Turkey in 1879. 8

Comtois
A draft horse from the Jura Mountains of France and Switzerland, the Comtois was used by Napoleon's army in the early 19th century. 17

Colorado Ranger

Connemara
From Connemara on the west coast of Ireland, this stocky little pony was once used by farmers to pull ploughs and transport turf from bogs. It is now a popular sports pony for children and adults alike. 10

Criollo
Found throughout South America, Criollos originate from the Andalusian horses brought by the Spanish when they first arrived there in the 16th century. 24

Dales Pony
A native mountain breed from the North of England, this tough pony was used by the British Army in both World Wars. 10

Danish Warmblood
Used as a showjumper, the Danish Warmblood is the newest of all the European warmblood breeds. 16

Dartmoor Pony
A gentle and calm breed, this small pony comes from Dartmoor in southwest England, where it still roams. It was once used in tin mines. 10

Dole Gudbrandsdal
The Dole was originally used in its native Norway as a packhorse on trade routes. 13

Dongola
Similar to the Barb and the Arabian, the Dongola is a riding horse from Sudan and Eritrea in Africa. Today it is popular in the Cameroon. 25

Dülmen Pony
The Dülmen is the only remaining native pony breed in Germany. 15

Dutch Harness
These horses are used in fine harness driving competitions, which feature light, refined horses with high stepping action. 12

Dutch Warmblood
Standing at 16 to 17 hands high, Dutch Warmbloods come in all solid colors. 17

English Thoroughbred
The English Thoroughbred was bred to race. It is used in flat racing, jump racing, showjumping, and dressage. 11, 26

Eriskay Pony
This kind and willing pony comes from the island of Eriskay, an area of the Outer Hebrides in northern Scotland. A rare breed, it is normally grey in color and its coat, mane, and tail are water-resistant. 9

Estonian
This breed is thought to be descended from forest horses that lived in Northern Europe five thousand years ago. 16

Exmoor Pony
A pony from southwest England, the Exmoor has existed since before Roman times. It is adapted to live in a wet climate, and has oily, water-repellent hair. 10

Falabella
At only eight hands high, this Argentinian horse is one of the smallest breeds in the world. 24

Faroe Pony
This pony exists only in the Faroe Islands, north of the United Kingdom. It grows a long, thick, water-resistant coat for the winter. 18

Fell Pony
The Fell Pony is native to the North of England. It was originally used to transport lead, iron, and coal over long distances. 9

Finnhorse
The national horse breed of Finland, this is one of the fastest and most versatile coldblood breeds in the world. Coldbloods are large horses that are bred for heavy, tiring labor such as agricultural work. 12

Fjord
From Norway, this ancient breed is characterized by its dun-colored coat and very thick mane, which is often two-tone and usually cut short. Vikings are believed to have used these horses. 16

Florida Cracker
Thought to be descended from horses brought to the Americas by the Spanish in the 1500s, the Florida Cracker was used mainly as a cattle horse. Its name comes from the sound a cowherd's whip makes. 4

Frederiksborger
Denmark's oldest breed, this rare horse is normally chestnut colored with white markings. It has a friendly and calm nature and is ideal for amateur riders. 13

Freiberger
This light draft horse was once used by farmers and soldiers as an artillery and packhorse. 18

Friesian
One of Europe's oldest breeds, from north of the Netherlands, this heavy black horse was used in Medieval times to carry knights into battle. It is now used for dressage, driving, and showing. 14, 26

Galiceno
Although it is small, the Galiceno is considered a horse and not a pony. This hardy Mexican breed can carry an adult all day, even in heat and over difficult terrain. 25

Gotland Pony
Sweden's only native pony, this breed lives on the small island of Gotland. 16

Hackney
Known as the "ballerina of the show ring," the Hackney is a driving horse known for pulling carriages. When it trots it brings its knees up high. 9

Haflinger
From the mountainous region of southern Austria and northern Italy, the Haflinger

Icelandic

is a small, sturdy, and energetic horse characterized by its chestnut coat. 13

Hanoverian
These German horses are known for their skill in dressage and showjumping. Many have won Olympic gold medals. 19

Heck
The Heck Horse was created by German zoologist brothers Lutz and Heinz Heck, who wanted to try to breed back the Tarpan, an extinct species of wild horse. 12

Hequ
These Chinese horses date back to the Tang dynasty, which began in the 7th century. 20

Highland Pony
Originally from the mountains of Scotland, the Highland Pony is hardy and well adapted to living in a harsh climate. 11

Holsteiner
Believed to be the oldest of the warmblood breeds, the Holsteiner has been bred in Schleswig-Holstein, Germany, for over seven hundred years. 13

Icelandic
The only horse breed native to Iceland, this small horse has five gaits: ambling and pace as well as walk, trot, and canter/gallop. This helps it to manoeuvre across harsh terrain. 15

Irish Draft
The Irish Draft was created in Ireland in the late 19th century as a farm horse. It worked the land during the week, went fox hunting on Saturdays, and pulled the family trap to church on Sundays. 11, 26

Irish Sport
This horse was created by breeding the Irish Draft with a Thoroughbred. Also known as the Irish Hunter, it is well known for its ability to jump. 11

Italian Heavy Draft
Bred mainly in the Veneto in northern Italy, the Italian Heavy Draft is usually chestnut with a flaxen mane and tail. 17

Java Pony
From Java in Indonesia, this pony is used mainly for farming, and is well adapted to the region's tropical climate. 23

Jeju
A Korean breed, the Jeju has such strong hooves that it does not need horseshoes. 21

Jutland
This compact draft horse from Denmark is known for pulling the brewery wagons of a famous beer brand. 16

Kabardin
From the Caucasus — which lie between the Caspian Sea and the Balkan Sea in Asia — Kabardins are known for their endurance, and are well adapted to living in mountains. 22

Kaimanawa
The Kaimanawa is a feral horse from New Zealand, a descendant of domestic horses that escaped into the wild. 25

Karabair
One of the most ancient breeds of central Asia, the Karabair is adapted to life in deserts and grass plains. 23

Karabakh
Normally chestnut or bay and known for its shiny coat, the Karabakh comes from the Caucasus — a region where Eastern Europe meets Western Asia. 20

Kathiawari
Like its close relative the Marwari horse from India, the Kathiawari has inward-pointing ears. It is normally chestnut in color. 23

Kentucky Mountain
Closely related to the Tennessee Walker, this calm-natured breed has a smooth gait that makes it easy to ride, even on rough terrain. 6

Kerry Bog Pony
From the west of Ireland, the Kerry Bog is a courageous and strong pony that was once used to help carry peat from bogs, and harvest seaweed from beaches. 10

Mountain Pleasure

Kiso
The Kiso comes from Japan. Although it is a small horse, it is bigger than many other native Japanese breeds. 21

Kladruber
A rare old breed from the Czech Republic, this horse is either black or grey. 15

Knabstrupper
This Danish breed has an unusual leopard-spotted coat. 19

Lipizzaner
Also known as the Lipizzan, this famous white breed is known for performing extraordinary "airs above the ground" dressage at the Spanish Riding School in Vienna, Austria. 18, 27

Lippitt Morgan
Descended from the Morgan breed, this horse is brown, chestnut, black, or bay in color. 5

Lokai
Bred by Uzbek tribes in Tajikistan in Asia, the Lokai was used as both a pack- and a riding horse. 20

Lusitano
This handsome horse takes it name from Lusitania, the ancient Roman name for what is now Portugal. 12

Mangalarga Marchador
Descended from the Portuguese Lusitano, this Brazilian horse has four gaits: walk, canter, and two ambling gaits. 24

Maremmano
Favored by Italian farmers and mounted police, the Maremmano were used in a successful cavalry charge in Russia on the Eastern Front during World War II. 19

Marsh Tacky
From South Carolina in the United States, the Marsh Tacky is adapted to working in boggy lowlands, and copes well with heat and humidity. 4

Marwari
The Marwari comes from Rajasthan in northern India and was once used as a cavalry horse. It has distinct inward-curving ears. 22

McCurdy Plantation
The McCurdy, like the Tennessee Walker and the Missouri Fox Trotter, is a gaited horse. This means that it has a number of natural movements, called gaits, that make it smooth to ride for long periods. 8

Menorquín
A black horse from the Spanish island of Menorca in the Mediterranean, the Menorquín is famous for taking part in the island's special style of dressage riding, *doma menorquina*. 19

Mérens
Native to the Pyrenees and the Ariégeois mountains of southern France, the Mérens is also known as the Ariégeois Pony, although it is a horse. It is always black. 13

Miniature
These horses cannot be ridden — even by children — but they are used for driving and in-hand classes over obstacle courses. 14

Misaki
A rare Japanese breed, the Misaki is dark-colored and small. 21

Missouri Fox Trotter
Developed in Missouri in the United States, this breed has a special gait called the fox trot, in which the diagonal front and back legs don't land at the same time. This creates a smooth ride. 7

Miyako
From the island of Miyako in Japan, the breed resembles the stocky Mongolian horse. 20

Mongolian
There are over three million of these horses in Mongolia. Believed to date back to the time of Genghis Khan — the 12th century — they are used for meat, milk, riding, and transport. 21

Morab
First developed in the United States in about 1800, the Morab is a mix of Arabian and Morgan breeds. A Morab called Goldust, one of the most famous trotting horses in history, won $10,000 in a race in 1861. 4

Morgan
One of the oldest breeds in the United States, Morgans are good riding and driving horses. They were used as cavalry horses by both sides during the American Civil War in the 1860s. 6

Mountain Pleasure
Known for its intelligence, this mountain horse is easy to train. It was originally bred in the 19th century to work in the mountains of Kentucky in the United States. 7

Moyle
The Moyle is unusual in having horny growths on its head. This rare breed was created by Rex Moyle, a Mormon, in the 1930s. 6

Murgese
Normally black or blue roan, the Murgese is a strong horse that comes from the south of Italy. 15

Mustang
Mustangs are free-roaming horses found in North America. They are descended from the first horses brought to the continent five hundred years ago by the Spanish. 4, 27

National Show Horse
Bred in the United States to compete in shows, the National Show Horse was created by mixing an Arabian with an American Saddlebred. 5

New Forest Pony
The New Forest Pony is strong enough to carry an adult as well as children. From the New Forest in the South of England, its origins are believed to go back to the Ice Age. 11

Newfoundland Pony
In the 17th and 18th centuries, British settlers to Newfoundland in North America brought horses with them to work the land. These hardy, intelligent ponies are their descendants. 8

Nokota
These horses once lived wild across the open ranges of North Dakota — hence the name. They are now used for fox hunting and showjumping. 6

Nordlandshest
A small breed from Norway, this horse was originally used on farms. 19

Noriker
One of Europe's oldest draft breeds, the powerful Noriker comes from Austria. 12

Norman Cob
From Normandy in northern France, this is a light breed of draft horse. 19

North American Single-Footing
A breed originating in the southern United States, the Single-Footing horse can move smoothly from slow up to a racing gait. 6

North Swedish
This cooperative Swedish breed is similar to the Norwegian Dole Gudbrandsdal. 14

Novokirghiz
The milk from this horse from Kyrgyzstan is used to make a fermented Asian drink called *kumis*. 22

Oldenburg
An excellent sports horse, this breed was created in the 17th century by the Counts of Oldenburg in northern Germany. 18

Orlov Trotter
The beautiful Orlov Trotter is an old Russian racing breed, renowned for its stamina. 21

Palomino
Palominos have amazing coloration: golden coats with white manes and tails. They have brown eyes, and the skin under their coats is dark. 8

Paso Fino
Also known as the Colombian Criolli Horse, the Paso Fino's name means "fine step" in Spanish. It earns this name because it moves with very little up-and-down motion. 4

Percheron
Originally used as a warhorse, the Percheron is a draft horse. Mainly grey or black, it is known for it docile nature even though it is very powerful. 15

Peruvian Paso
The Peruvian is a smooth-gaited horse from Peru in South America. It has a big, ground-covering stride, which is ideal for trekking long distances over mountains. 25

Pottok
An ancient breed of horse from Europe's Basque Country, the Pottok is the official mascot of France's Bayonne rugby team. 19

Przewalski's Horse
A wild horse from Central Asia, the Przewalski is stocky with short legs and a mane that stands straight up. 20

Racking Horse
Known as the Racking Horse because "rack" is an old-fashioned term for gait, it is well known for its comfortable ride. It was once used by plantation owners in North America. 6

Rocky Mountain
From the Appalachian mountains in eastern Kentucky, this horse is popular for pleasure, trail, and endurance riding. 7

Russian Don
Used as a cavalry horse by the Cossacks, this breed comes from the steppes (flat grasslands) near Russia's river Don. 23

Shire

Russian Trotter
The Russian Trotter was created by mixing the American Trotter with the Orlov Trotter. 21

Selle Français
The name Selle Français translates as French Saddle. A lightweight breed for riding only, this horse is an excellent jumper. 13

Shagya Arabian
In 1947, the American World War II general George S. Patton brought the first two Shagyas, Pilot and Gazall II, to America from Europe. 19

Shetland Pony
This is a small, hardy pony, originally from the Shetland Islands in northern Scotland. Its strength and hardiness help it to survive the harsh winters there. 11, 27

Shire
One of the world's tallest breeds, the Shire can pull huge, heavy loads and carts with ease. 10

Sorraia
This very rare breed of horse, now the focus of conservation efforts, is indigenous to the Sorraia River basin in Portugal. 18

Spanish Jennet Horse
This horse has been bred to recreate the Jennet, a small, light riding horse that was used in Medieval Europe. It is known for its pleasant disposition and well-muscled stature. 14

Spanish Mustang
These horses are believed to have been brought to North America by Spanish explorers in the 1500s. 15

Spotted Saddle
A popular trail horse, the Spotted Saddle comes from Tennessee in the United States. It does not trot, but instead has a smooth four-beat gait. 6

Standardbred
Believed to be the fastest harness horse in the world, the Standardbred is similar to its ancestor, the Thoroughbred. 5

Suffolk Punch
From Suffolk in the east of England, this is a heavy draft horse that used to work on farms in the 19th century. It is always chestnut in color. 10

Swedish Warmblood
Normally chestnut, brown, or bay in color, the Swedish Warmblood is used for dressage, three-day eventing, and showjumping. 17

Tennessee Walker
Developed in the Southern United States in the 18th century to use on farms and plantations, this horse has a smooth gait that makes it comfortable to ride over long distances. 7, 27

Tersk
The Tersk, a Russian breed, looks very similar to the Arabian, but is a bit taller. 23

Trakehner
From Germany, this horse was developed as a cavalry horse by the King of Prussia in the 18th century. It is considered to be the Thoroughbred of the warmblood breeds. 13

Vyatka
A rare breed from Russia, the Vyatka was used to pull troikas — large snow sleighs — in teams of three. 22

Welsh Cob Pony
Originally bred in the Middle Ages to work on farms in Wales, this tall pony is now used mainly as a show horse. It is known for its gentle and obedient nature. 9

Welsh Mountain Pony
The Welsh Mountain Pony is believed to have existed in the British Isles in Celtic times, before the Romans invaded two thousand years ago. 9

Westphalian
Known for being calm, reliable, and friendly, this German warmblood horse is one of the most successful breeds in equestrian sport. 18

Württemberger
One of Germany's showjumping and dressage breeds, the Württemberger has an excellent temperament. 17

Yonaguni
This rare breed of small horse comes from the remote Yonaguni Island, which is situated far south of the main islands of Japan. 21

Lipizzaner Foal

A FIREFLY BOOK

Published by Firefly Books Ltd. 2018
Copyright © 2018 Eight Books Ltd.
Text copyright © 2018 Mark Fletcher
Illustrations copyright © 2018 Jim Medway

All rights reserved. No part of this publication may be reproduced, stored in a retrieval
system or transmitted in any form or by any means, electronic, mechanical, photocopying,
recording or otherwise, without the written permission of the Publisher.

First Printing

Publisher Cataloging-in-Publication Data (U.S.)

Library of Congress Control Number: 2018933321

Library and Archives Canada Cataloguing in Publication

Medway, Jim, author
        Big horses, little horses : a visual guide to the world's horses & ponies/ Jim Medway.
Includes index.
ISBN 978-0-228-10109-3 (hardcover)
        1. Horse breeds--Pictorial works--Juvenile literature. 2. Horses--
Pictorial works--Juvenile literature. 3. Horse breeds--Juvenile literature.
4. Horses--Juvenile literature. I. Title. II. Title: Visual guide to the
world's horses and ponies.
SF302.M44 2018   j636.1   C2018-900874-1

Published in Canada by
Firefly Books Ltd.
50 Staples Avenue, Unit 1
Richmond Hill, Ontario L4B 0A7

Published in the United States by
Firefly Books (U.S.) Inc.
P.O. Box 1338, Ellicott Station
Buffalo, New York, USA 14205

Printed in China